9/05

$18.96

The London Tower Bridge

by Margaret Speaker Yuan

BLACKBIRCH®
PRESS

San Diego • Detroit • New York • San Franciso • Cleveland • New Haven, Conn. • Waterville, Maine • London • Munich

For more information, contact
The Gale Group, Inc.
27500 Drake Rd.
Farmington Hills, MI 48331-3535
Or you can visit our Internet site at http://www.gale.com

LIBRARY OF CONGRESS CATALOGING-IN-PUBLICATION DATA

Yuan, Margaret Speaker
  The London Tower Bridge / by Margaret Speaker Yuan.
    p. cm. — (Building world landmarks)
Summary: Describes the techniques used and difficulties faced building the London Tower Bridge
Includes bibliographical references and index.
  ISBN 1-4103-0323-3 (hardback : alk. paper)

Printed in the United States
10 9 8 7 6 5 4 3 2 1

Table of Contents

Introduction
The Wonder Bridge 5

Chapter 1
London and the Thames 9

Chapter 2
The Bridge Begins 17

Chapter 3
Bascules, Chains, and Steam Engines 25

Chapter 4
Symbol of a City 35

Notes 44

Chronology 45

Glossary 46

For More Information 47

Index 48

The Wonder Bridge

THE TOWER BRIDGE spans the Thames River between the London Docklands and the London Bridge. On the north bank of the river, the bridge adjoins the historic Tower of London, which was established as a fortress soon after William the Conqueror invaded England in 1066. In the centuries that followed, London grew from a medieval village into one of the world's greatest cities.

As London's population increased, the Thames became one of the world's busiest shipping channels. By the 1860s, numerous bridges crossed the Thames. Due to the heavy traffic, which included horse-drawn vehicles, riders, and pedestrians, another bridge was needed. For nearly two decades, from the 1860s to the 1880s, many sites and designs were suggested for a new bridge. Finally, in 1885, Horace Jones, the city architect, proposed a unique design that would balance

Opposite:
Spanning the Thames River, the Tower Bridge is a well-known symbol of London and one of the most recognizable bridges in the world.

5

the transportation needs of the city's inhabitants with the shipping needs of the river commerce.

In Jones's design, masonry turrets and parapets disguised the structural steel towers that supported the Tower Bridge's roadway. Graceful suspension chains hung from the towers to the riverbanks on the north and south sides of the bridge. The roadway to each tower was supported by the suspension chains. At the towers, the roadway changed from the suspension spans to the bascule (the French word for "seesaw") sections of the bridge. When ships needed to sail upriver, the bascules swung upward to allow them safe passage.

When it opened in 1894, the Tower Bridge was the largest and most technically advanced bridge in the world. In the century that has passed since its construction, "the Wonder Bridge" has weathered the

change from steam-powered to electric operations, and from horse-powered vehicles to the internal combustion engine. At the same time, the unique profile and distinctive design of the Tower Bridge have come to symbolize the city of London.

When the Tower Bridge opened in 1894, it was the largest bridge in the world.

LONDRES

London and the Thames

RECORDS OF A bridge across the Thames are found as early as A.D. 80. Built of wood, the bridge soon fell into disrepair and was replaced by a ferry. As the centuries passed, other timber bridges were erected. The first stone bridge was the London Bridge, which was completed in 1209. For most of its six-century lifetime, it was the only bridge that connected the city of London on the north to the south bank of the Thames. Congestion on the bridge became so bad that in 1722, all traffic was ordered to keep to the left. This order became the established rule of the road throughout England.

The Industrial Revolution produced vast changes in the economy of Britain. By the nineteenth century, workers began to move away from farms to the cities, where they could find employment in factories. Housing was often cheaper south of the Thames, but jobs were located north of the river. Workers crossed the river by

Opposite:
As shown in this eighteenth-century engraving, boats and ships of all sizes transported goods and passengers along the Thames River.

ferry or by the London Bridge. New bridges were built in the 1800s, but London Bridge remained the most congested one. The new bridges were west of London Bridge, and the closest one was a half-mile away. For people without carriages or horses, crossing the Thames meant either a slow walk through the crowds at London Bridge or a hike of a mile or more round-trip to one of the other bridges. These alternatives were unattractive, especially in the frigid London winters.

A new bridge was needed, but no decision could be reached about where to locate it, who should construct it, and what its design should be. Many public agencies were involved in the debate. The fact that London had no citywide government, but only a loose coalition of governing bodies, compounded the difficulty of the decision. Not only was the Corporation of London (the oldest municipal body in the city) involved, but also the Metropolitan Board of Works (the city's public works agency), as well as Parliament (the United Kingdom's national elected body). The Corporation of London's analysis of where people lived, where they worked, and how far they would have to walk to the new bridge led to the selection of a site at Tower Hill, close to the Tower of London.

A Design Challenge

The bridge's design posed a challenge. Ocean-going vessels laden with grain, wool, cotton, ivory, silver, tea, and myriad other goods docked along the river between Tower Hill and the London Bridge. Barges brought coal to be burned in furnaces or fireplaces in

The Tower of London

William, duke of Normandy, invaded England in 1066. Following the Battle of Hastings, he was crowned ruler of Britain and was known afterwards as William the Conqueror. In order to subdue the Anglo-Saxons who inhabited most of England, he took over and strengthened a Roman fort on a hill near London. In the years following the conquest, William built a stone tower on the site of his initial fortifications. A symbol of the monarchy's power, the Tower of London served as a stronghold and refuge for the royal family in times of civil strife. It is recognized worldwide as the best-preserved medieval castle in Europe.

Over the centuries, more towers, a curtain wall, a chapel, a moat, and other buildings were added to the site. The tower was used as a prison, and was the site of seven executions, including those of three English queens. In 1483, the twelve-year-old king Edward V and his brother Richard were imprisoned in the Tower by their uncle Richard, duke of Gloucester. The two boys disappeared, and it is popularly believed that they were murdered by their uncle, who assumed the throne as Richard III.

The crown jewels of Britain are on display in the tower, and include crowns,

Originally built as a symbol of power by William the Conquerer, the Tower of London now holds the crown jewels of Britain.

jewelry, scepters, swords, and coronation robes. King Henry VIII's armor is on display as well.

When the Tower Bridge was designed, the site's historic significance was a major consideration. Horace Jones sought to integrate the bridge design into the existing architecture. Many people, viewing the Tower Bridge and the Tower of London, have found it easy to believe that they were built at about the same time. Although this popular belief is an engineering impossibility, because the steel to construct the bridge was not available during the time of the construction of the tower, it serves to demonstrate the success of Jones's design.

Horace Jones's Victorian Gothic design (pictured) hid the bridge's machinery within two towers.

the winter. Small ships that carried cargo and passengers sailed up and down the river. Unless the new bridge were designed to permit the ships to pass under it, the docks west of Tower Hill would be forced to close. If the bridge were tall enough for shipping, it would be difficult for both pedestrians and horse-drawn vehicles to climb the steep grade such a high structure would require.

In 1884, a select committee of the House of Commons (which together with the House of Lords, make up Parliament, the United Kingdom's ruling body) met to consider the question of the bridge design. Numerous designs were presented to the committee. Many of them were complicated in concept and difficult, if not impossible, to build and operate. Finally, a proposal was presented for a drawbridge that opened in the center.

The Design Is Chosen

The idea of a drawbridge gained support as the debate continued in the committee. Horace Jones, the city architect, presented a plan that attracted favorable attention. He proposed a seesaw, or bascule, bridge. This design featured two girders, called bascules, that could be raised upward until they were nearly perpendicular to the roadway. The design allowed a wide channel for tall ships as well as for the many smaller craft that plied the Thames. With the bascules closed, pedestrians and carriage traffic would ascend a very mild grade, or incline, as the roadway passed over the river. This feature was an important safety consideration, because in wet or icy conditions, horses, carriages, and pedestrians might slip on a steep incline. In addition, the bridge would feature two high-level walkways for pedestrians, accessible by both stairs and elevators. The walkways would be set so high above the river that ships could pass beneath them. Pedestrian traffic could therefore continue across the walkways when the bascules of the bridge were opened for shipping.

Jones's design incorporated architectural details that made the bridge a masterpiece in the style known as Victorian Gothic. Named for Britain's ruler, Queen Victoria, and for its use of elements from Gothic cathedrals, fortresses, and other medieval buildings, Victorian Gothic was the most popular architectural style in the world during the second half of the nineteenth century.

The Victorian Gothic design hid the bridge machinery and most of the structural steel in two tall stone-covered towers. Turrets, parapets, gargoyles, and other stone carvings decorated the towers. The towers, the high-level walkways, and the lowered bascules together formed a rectangle-shaped gateway to the city, as seen from the river. The stonework decorations on top of the towers crowned the corners of the rectangular frame and drew attention to the suspension chains. The suspension chains made a delicate, graceful contrast to the strong central rectangle. Not only was the design functional, serving the needs of all types of traffic, along, above, and across the river, it was widely admired for its beauty. Most important of all, the Victorian Gothic style of the design matched the medieval architecture of the Tower of London.

A Question of Power

One further question was considered before the design could be approved. To lift the bascules would require steam engines larger and more powerful than any previously built. The committee required confirmation that such enormous steam engines could be built, and that the bascules could be raised and lowered safely in the calculated time frame (five minutes, on average, to open the bascules, allow a ship to pass, and close the bascules).

Jones answered this issue in consultation with the eminent engineer John Wolfe-Barry. Wolfe-Barry's experience included engineering work on the London Underground, on Southwark Bridge, on the Charing

Cross Railroad, and on many other projects. Wolfe-Barry in turn consulted a number of fellow engineers. Their consensus, which agreed with Wolfe-Barry's opinion, was that the plan was thoroughly workable.

The committee reported its findings to the House of Commons. A bill was drawn up and considered in both the House of Commons and the House of Lords. The bill passed, and on August 14, 1885, Queen Victoria signed it. The new bridge had been approved.

Each of the bridge's bascules (pictured) could be raised and lowered by steam engines to allow ships to pass.

The Bridge Begins

THE BRIDGE'S DESIGN called for two enormous piers, each more than two hundred feet tall, to be sunk into the riverbed. The piers were the foundations for two towers that would support the suspension chains, the high-level walkways, and the bascules with their operating machinery. Two abutments, structures on which to anchor the suspension chains, would be constructed between the towers and the riverbanks. The suspension chains would support the roadway up to the towers. At the towers, the roadway would cross over the bascules. A special hinged flap that locked into place when the bascules were lowered ensured that there was no gap in the roadway. When the bascules were raised, the flap swung flat against the bascule. On the southern approach to the bridge, an engine house would be built to hold the boilers

Opposite:
Construction on the Tower Bridge began in 1886, after Jones and engineer John Wolfe-Barry had solved the project's unique design challenges.

that would provide the steam power to operate the bascules.

The bridge would operate on the seesaw principle. A seesaw is usually a long plank that balances on a pin, called a pivot, which goes into a hole drilled through the plank. When weight is applied to one end of the seesaw, the plank rotates on the pivot and the opposite end goes up. When the weight is lifted from the end of the plank, the plank goes back to the horizontal position. For the bridge, instead of a long plank, the bascules would be steel structures weighing more than one thousand tons, or about the same as eighty-five elephants.

The pivot for the bascule would be a steel pin that ran the width of the bascule. Each bascule would be balanced at rest, and would swing upward on its pivot when weight was applied to its landward end.

Early Challenges

Before construction could begin on the piers, unique challenges had to be solved by both the architect and the engineer. River traffic would continue to sail along the waterway during the bridge's construction. The act of Parliament that authorized the bridge also defined many details of the construction. Because the Thames experienced tidal changes in the water level, measurements had to be made when the tide was highest, the point called the high-water mark. The width of the shipping channel, both during construction and after the bridge was completed (200 feet [61 meters] after construction, 160 [49 meters] during construction)

was defined. Temporary wooden scaffolding would extend beyond the riverside edge of each pier for more than forty feet (12 meters) into the shipping channel, so the piers could not be constructed at the same time. This requirement, although it was well justified by the amount of shipping that passed along the river, meant that the construction took longer than it would have if the piers had been constructed simultaneously.

There was little room for storage of construction materials near the site, so the iron, stone, wood, and steel needed to build the bridge were shipped in small quantities. Coal, used to power the machinery on the site, was also shipped and stored in small quantities. For more than eight months, from August 1885 to April 1886, John Wolfe-Barry and Horace Jones drew

River traffic, which continued on the Thames while the bridge was being built, slowed construction.

up plans for construction, such as the plans for the temporary wooden scaffolds and the iron work used in the construction of the piers. Together, they hired contractors to provide the building materials.

Work Begins

Thirty feet beneath the surface of the Thames, work to prepare the site for construction began. Dressed in leather suits topped by metal helmets, and connected by air tubes to the surface, divers leveled the surface of the riverbed. On barges above them, other workers riv-

Divers worked thirty feet underwater to level the surface of the riverbed.

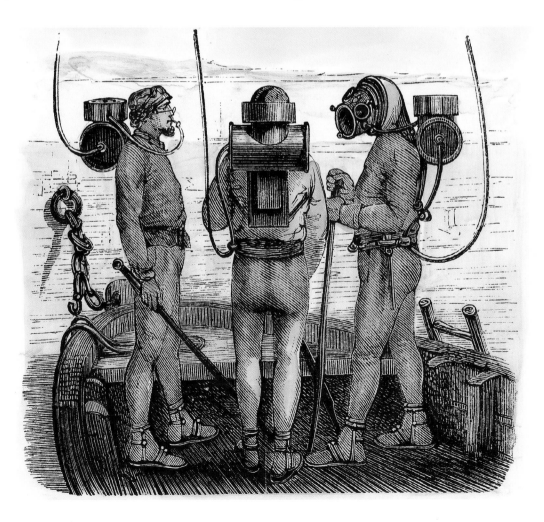

eted huge panels of wrought iron into open-ended, watertight boxes known as the permanent caissons. The bottom edges of each caisson were sharpened, and reinforced with extra-strong wrought iron. The caissons were hung from a temporary wooden scaffold and lowered into the water. When a caisson reached the riverbed, the sharp edge helped it begin to sink into the soil. As each caisson sank, workers stationed on the wooden scaffold controlled the angle of the caisson to make sure it went straight down. Screws at the top of the scaffolding were turned to apply pressure to the caissons and force them into the soil. When the top edges of the permanent caissons approached the high-water mark, workers riveted additional panels to them, known as the temporary caissons. The temporary caissons kept water from flowing over the tops of the permanent caissons.

Divers inside the caisson excavated the riverbed gravel, which was hauled up by a crane and taken away in barges. About twenty feet below the surface of the riverbed, the caissons reached the London clay, a firm layer underneath the gravel and loose soil of the riverbed. The clay was hard and uniform in texture, and it was watertight. It would be the foundation upon which the enormous weight of each tower would rest.

Once each caisson had sunk about ten feet into the watertight clay layer, workers at the top of the caisson stopped applying pressure to the screws so that the caisson did not sink any further. The water inside it was pumped out, and the remaining digging took place in dry conditions. Workers excavated an additional five to ten feet (three meters) of clay below the lower edge of the caisson. They cut outward for a distance of five feet (one and a half meters) on three of the four sides of this additional excavation. The outward cuts, called undercuttings, served to increase the surface area that had been excavated below the bottom edge of each caisson. When the adjoining caissons were constructed, the undercuttings of one caisson connected with the undercuttings of its neighboring caissons. The linked undercuttings, when filled with concrete, would create a continuous foundation that flared five feet outward from the bases of the excavations. The fact that the foundation would be continuous and broad increased the stability of the pier.

Stable Foundations

Twelve caissons per pier were constructed. They were positioned so that there would be a large central rectangle with the caissons around it. Eight caissons, four to a side, created the long side of the rectangle. Two caissons were placed on each of the narrow ends of the rectangle.

Once all the caissons had been created, concrete was poured into them. The concrete filled the undercuttings and the excavations below the bottom edges of the caissons as well as the caissons themselves. Workers pumped the central rectangle dry, and lined it with masonry, which included granite, brickwork, and concrete. They left room inside the rectangle for the steel pillars that would form the towers—for the landward ends of the bascules—and for the bascule machinery. Once the masonry lining of the rectangle

Two enormous piers (pictured) were sunk deep into the riverbed to support the towers on each end of the bridge.

was finished, the last step in completing the piers was taken. The temporary caissons were removed. The completed piers, which were waterproof and strong enough to resist the pressure of the river's currents, extended from the tops of the permanent caissons up to the position where the roadway would be built. Work could now begin on the steel structures of the towers, on the bascules, and on the steam engines that would lift the bascules.

Bascules, Chains, and Steam Engines

THREE TECHNICAL ACHIEVEMENTS combine to make the bridge an engineering marvel: the bascules, the chains, and the steam engines. All three elements were built on a scale never before seen, and gave the bridge its contemporary nickname: "the Wonder Bridge."

Deep inside the piers, workers began to build the steel pillars that would support the roadways and bascules. The contract for providing the structural steel had been given to William Arrol and Company, a firm that was a leader both in the quality of the steel it produced and in worker safety programs. Manufactured at Arrol's Dalmarnock Iron Works in Scotland, steel was shipped to London and transferred to river barges near the construction site. Steel segments up to five tons in weight could be shipped and transferred easily. At the site, cranes moved the steel segments into the piers, where workers riveted them together to

Opposite:
The bridge design included two towers, suspension chains, high-level walkways, and a roadway covering the bascules.

The crews that built the high-level walkways (pictured) worked along wooden scaffolding without safety nets, hard hats, or safety shoes.

make steel pillars. In the course of a ten-hour day, a crew of steelworkers could set about two hundred rivets by hand.

With wide, octagonal-shaped bases, the steel pillars, four per tower, would extend up to the level of the suspension chains. The two riverward pillars of each tower would support the high-level footways, while the two shoreward pillars support the suspension chains. Each pillar was bolted to a massive granite slab set into the concrete foundation of the piers. Between the pillars, the bridge design called for space to accommodate the public stairs, for the elevators that would carry passengers to the high-level walkways, and for the landward end of each of the bascules, which would swing downward when the bridge was opened.

Walkways and Suspension Chains

Once the pillars were in place, workers began the construction of the high-level walkways and the suspension chains. Wooden scaffolding supported the walkway's horizontal beams as the workers riveted them into place. Working 150 feet (46 meters) above the river, without safety nets, crews riveted steel sections, called cantilevers, from each of the towers toward the center of the bridge. Cantilevers are sections of a bridge that are supported at one end and that can bear weight along their length. The walkway cantilevers would support the weight of the pedestrians once the bridge was completed. Contemporary drawings show the workers, without hard hats or safety shoes, as they crouched or crawled along the wooden scaffolding to set the rivets into the beams.

A central section linked the two cantilevers together. The difficulty of making the steel join accurately had been addressed in advance. A trial construction at the ironworks in Scotland ensured that all the pieces of the steel puzzle fit together without problems. With the walkways across the river in place, building the suspension chains could begin.

Two abutments, structures which would support the landward ends of the suspension chains, were

While some workers built the walkways, other crews constructed the two abutments that would support the suspension chains.

constructed between the towers and the riverbank while the high-level walkways were being built. The weight that would be supported by the abutments was much less than the weight supported by the piers, so the abutments were smaller, weighed less, and were easier to construct than the piers.

Building the chains themselves was a difficult task. They weighed approximately one ton per linear foot, meaning each foot weighed about the same amount as an average automobile. The wooden trestles built to support them during construction had to be very strong and stable, both to carry the weight of the chains and to keep them from swinging in the wind as the workers riveted sections of the chains into place. From the abutments, land ties of steel were strung to the shore where they were firmly set in concrete blocks. The land ties provided additional stability and kept the bridge from moving in windy conditions.

From each chain, workers installed a series of steel suspension rods, which hung downwards. Cross girders connected corresponding suspension rods on each side of the bridge. Between the cross girders, workers laid short longitudinal (lengthwise) girders, and then corrugated steel plates, which would be paved over to form the fixed portion of the span.

While the chains were being constructed, the moving sections of the bridge were also being built. Each

The bridge's suspension chains weigh about one ton per linear foot.

of the two bascule sections would be formed from four main longitudinal girders that would run lengthwise and support the roadway. Cross girders would be built across the longitudinal girders, and steel plates, called the roadway plates, would be built along the cross girders. The road surface would be laid across the roadway plates.

The Bascules

Workers built the longitudinal girders, with the cross girders and the plates, to a length of forty feet out over the river. They threaded the pivot, the pin on which the bascule would rotate, through the longitudinal girders. On the landward side of the bascule, they built the balancing section, called the counterbalance. If the bascule were an enormous seesaw, the counterbalance would be where one seat, the landward seat, was located. Instead of a seat that would lie flat on the bascule, two sets of huge steel teeth, like enormous gears, were bolted vertically around the end of the counterbalance. The teeth fitted into corresponding teeth of the steam engine's gears. When steam pressure was sent into the engine, the gears would turn. As they turned, the gears would press the corresponding teeth on the counterbalance. This pressure would force the landward end of the bascule downward, thereby raising the roadway end. When the steam pressure was released, the bascule would move back up into its closed, or horizontal, position.

Since the engines had not yet been put into place inside the towers, the bascules were rotated upward

Steam and Steel

Two technological advances made the Tower Bridge possible. One was the steam engine, and the other was the Bessemer converter.

Steam power is the power that makes a kettle whistle. When water comes to a boil inside a kettle, the liquid water turns into water vapor, also known as steam. If the steam is forced out through a small hole, the kettle whistles. If the kettle were sealed, the pressure of the water would build up. Because it would not have room to expand and become steam, the water would remain liquid instead of becoming water vapor. The water pressure would have the strength to do more than whistle when the heated water was used to power an engine. Depending on the size of the sealed kettle, called a boiler, the pressurized water could lift and lower an elevator, or it could be used to operate the bascules of the Tower Bridge.

The steam engine was invented about a century before the bridge was constructed. The engines that operated the Tower Bridge were the largest, most advanced steam engines in the world.

Without high-quality, bulk production of steel, the bridge would have been much more expensive and difficult to build. Until the middle of the 1800s, steel was created in batches of forty or fifty pounds

The Bessemer converter dramatically cut the time and cost required to make steel.

at the largest. The Bessemer converter, patented in 1856, allowed steelmakers to produce batches of steel that ranged from four tons in early models to later examples that could create thirty tons of steel at a time. Named for its inventor, Henry Bessemer, the Bessemer converter took molten iron, mixed it with oxygen, and burned off the impurities at a high temperature. This process converted iron into steel. The converter cut the cost and the time of steel production significantly.

The advances in steel and steam technology helped the Tower Bridge earn its nickname, "the Wonder Bridge."

using a small steam-powered crank. The remaining portion of each bascule, an additional seventy feet (twenty-one meters), was erected while the bascules were in their upraised position.

The Steam Engines Go In

William Armstrong designed the Tower Bridge's steam engines.

While the bascules were being constructed, workers inside the towers installed the steam engines. The engines for the Tower Bridge were designed by William Armstrong, one of the leading hydraulic power specialists in the world. Built and tested at Armstrong's machine works in Newcastle, on the northwest coast of England, the engines were shipped by sea to London. They were installed in pairs that could be operated independently. This feature increased the bridge's safety. If an engine failed for any reason, one of the backup engines could be activated immediately to prevent the bascules from swinging out of control.

The steam engines actually used pressurized, heated water rather than steam. Four coal-powered boilers, each seven and one-half feet in diameter and thirty feet long, were brought up the river by barge and lifted by cranes into the engine house on the south side of the bridge. The boilers burned coal to heat water. The water was heated inside a closed container so that it could not expand to become steam. The boilers heated water

to a pressure of 850 pounds per square inch (60 kg/cm). To explain how much force is exerted inside the boiler, Wolfe-Barry noted in his essay on the Tower Bridge that a typical locomotive engine's boiler would usually have a pressure of about 170 pounds per square inch (12 kg/cm), or one-fifth of the pressure inside the bridge's boilers. The pressurized water was carried through a series of pipes to each of the towers, where it was used to power the steam engines. Painted green, with red, black, and gold trim, the Tower Bridge's steam engines were the largest of their kind in the world.

With the bridge near completion, its distinctive profile had taken shape. Only the masonry exterior with its crowning decorations remained to be finished.

The engines, which used pressurized heated water instead of steam, were the largest in the world.

Chapter 4

Symbol
of a City

THE DECORATIONS OF the towers had begun after most of the steel infrastructure was completed. The stonework was organized so that it did not interfere with the remaining construction on the site. Stonework continued as the workers built the high-level walkways, the bascules, the suspension chains, and the steam engines.

The stonework served to crown the structure and give it unity of design with the nearby Tower of London. Granite came from a quarry in Cornwall, in the southwestern part of England. Stone was cut at the quarry and finished according to where it would be positioned on the tower. At the bridge, stone workers stood on platforms that hung from wire ropes. They completed the elaborate openwork carvings that reached nineteen feet (six meters) in height above the rooftops of the towers.

Finishing touches, such as the gaslamps that would light the bridge, as well as the elevators, decorative

Opposite:
The London Tower Bridge took eight years and about 1 million pounds sterling, or $110 million today, to build.

THE CORPORATION OF THE CITY OF LONDON.

Opening of **THE TOWER BRIDGE**, June 30, 1894.
BY
H.R.H. THE PRINCE of WALES. K.G.
ON BEHALF OF
HER MAJESTY THE QUEEN.

THE RIGHT HON^{BLE} GEORGE ROBERT TYLER, Lord Mayor.

JOHN VOCE MOORE ESQ^R ALDERMAN.
JOSEPH COCKFIELD DIMSDALE ESQ^R ALDERMAN. } Sheriffs.

ADMIT *Arthur Goulston Esq and Lady*

Albert J. Altman
CHAIRMAN.

An invitation from the Corporation of the City of London announced the opening ceremony of the London Tower Bridge.

panels for the high-level walkways, and, most importantly, the roadway paving, continued through the spring of 1894. The steam engines were tested, as was the strength of the bascules in their lowered position. A few days before the opening ceremonies, carts loaded with 150 tons (136 metric tons) of material were moved onto the bascules. The deflection, or downward curve, of the roadway was measured and found to be insignificant, at just over 1.5 inches (38 millimeters). With the testing completed, the bridge was ready for opening day.

Opening Day

"Saturday, June 30, 1894 was the perfect English summer day,"[1] according to contemporary accounts. After decades of discussion and planning and eight years of

Prices and Wages

During the time the Tower Bridge was built, the English unit of currency was the pound sterling. Pounds were also units of weight.

There were 20 shillings to the pound, and a loaf of bread cost on average about 1 shilling. Laborers earned between forty to sixty pounds sterling per year, while workers in skilled trades (builders, shipwrights, or stone workers) earned around one hundred pounds sterling per year, or about 38.5 shillings per week. People ate about a pound of bread per day, so a family of four spent a shilling a day on bread. A family of four with one skilled wage-earner spent more than one-fifth of its income on bread alone. As a result, in most families, everyone, including children, had to work to afford food, clothing, and housing.

Laborers, working 150 feet above the river with no safety nets, earned between forty and sixty pounds sterling in a year.

On June 30, 1894, Londoners jammed the shores of the Thames and crowded into boats on the river to celebrate the bridge's opening.

work, Londoners were ready to celebrate their newest bridge. Flags, bunting, and flowers decorated the span. Spectators lined the Thames and crowded onto every kind of boat, barge, ferry, or watercraft that they could find. The ceremonial procession, headed by the prince and princess of Wales, arrived at noon. Mounted guards preceded the royals, while carriages carrying James Wolfe-Barry, the sheriffs of London, and the lord mayor of the city, followed them. The prince of Wales declared the bridge open while the national anthem was played by massed bands. When the prince of Wales activated the bascules, silence fell on the crowd. More than one thousand tons of steel per bascule swung upward. In ninety seconds, the bascules were open.

Cannons sounded from the tower, and the crowd drowned the gunfire with their cheers. HMS *Landrail* sailed up the river through the bridge, followed by a river procession that included representatives of the House of Commons, the London County Council, Lloyd's Insurance, the Watermen's Company, and many other institutions. The celebration lasted well into the night.

Costly, Yet Affordable

By the time the bridge was finished, Wolfe-Barry estimated that it had cost about 1 million pounds sterling. In today's currency, that would be about $110 million. The construction was financed by an ancient charity, the Bridge House Estates Trust. For centuries, the Bridge House Estates Trust had collected rent from stores and houses on the old London Bridge. The money was lent or given away to charitable causes, such as hospitals for the poor, and for the construction of roadways and bridges. As Wolfe-Barry noted, "The whole of the expense will be defrayed out of the funds carefully husbanded by the Bridge House Estates Trust. Londoners will thus be presented, without the charge of one penny, with a free bridge. The expense of working the bridge . . . will also be paid."[2] For many working-class Londoners, being able to get to work without paying tolls was an important financial aid.

In the bridge's first year, the bascules were raised 6,160 times. Sixty thousand pedestrians and eight thousand horse-drawn vehicles crossed the bridge. As the years passed, the pedestrian traffic on the high-level walkways decreased. There were fewer pedestrians in general on the bridge, and many pedestrians also chose to wait while the bascules were raised. The operators of the bridge noted that the spectacular sight of the bascules in motion, and of ships passing along the waterway, was worth the five-minute delay. By 1910, the high-level walkways were closed.

Into the Twentieth Century

In the early 1900s, a new type of vehicle began to appear. The invention of the automobile meant new challenges for the bridge. Gasoline- or diesel-fueled engines replaced draft horses. Vehicular traffic across the bridge skyrocketed. The speed of the automobile traffic, and the weight of the vehicles, proved to be much greater than that of horse-drawn carriages. The bridge operators were concerned that the vibration from so many vehicles going so fast would damage or undermine the bridge. The bridge's solid foundations, durable construction, and steel framework, however, proved equal to the new challenges for more than a century.

For eighty years, from its opening until the mid-1970s, the bridge was operated by steam power. As river traffic diminished, the bridge opened less frequently. The number of times the bascules were raised declined to about nine hundred per year. Although a proposal was made to leave the bascules permanently lowered, there was still enough river traffic to justify opening them. The decision was made to replace the power source for the machinery to raise the bascules. Steam power was replaced with electric power when

From Horses to Automobiles

The year that construction began on the Tower Bridge, 1886, Gottlieb Daimler produced the first four-wheeled, gasoline-powered automobile. By the time the bridge opened in 1894, automobiles were being built in several European countries and the United States.

Internal combustion engines typically burn either gasoline or diesel fuel. The fuel is ignited inside the engine, unlike steam engines, where the fuel is burned in a furnace outside the engine. Internal combustion engines, produced on assembly lines, proved to be less expensive and more reliable than horses.

Although horses provided the power for most vehicles from 1894 through the early 1920s, the rise of the internal combustion engine meant that traffic increased on the bridge. The new vehicles traveled faster than horse-drawn carriages. More traffic at higher speeds meant more total weight and more vibration on the bridge.

Today, as many as 150,000 vehicles per day cross the Tower Bridge, most of

While cars and buses have replaced horse-drawn carriages, the bridge has not had to undergo any major structural changes.

them powered by internal combustion engines. Few structures built in the nineteenth century have withstood a similar increase in traffic without major structural changes or substantial damage. The steel framework of the bridge, combined with its solid foundations in the London clay, have proved equal to the challenges presented by the increases in traffic caused by new types of vehicles.

the bridge was renovated in 1976. In 1977, the bridge was painted red, white, and blue to celebrate Queen Elizabeth II's silver jubilee, the twenty-fifth anniversary of her coronation.

The bridge was established as an education center in 1982. The high-level pedestrian walkways were re-opened, and the original Victorian engine rooms were opened to the public for the first time. In-depth, multilingual, interactive descriptions explain many of the operating details of the bridge.

In 2000, cracks and signs of wear were found in parts of the bridge. A major refurbishment of the bridge was needed. In October 2002, the bridge was closed for thirty-nine days as crews worked around the clock to

The Tower Bridge's bascules, which now run on electric power, still open for ships to pass even though shipping along the Thames has diminished.

Every day more than 150,000 vehicles cross the Tower Bridge, an architectural icon of the city of London.

complete the repairs. Currently, as many as 150,000 vehicles cross the bridge every day.

The Tower Bridge remains a vital link for commuters between the north and south banks of the Thames River. The bascules still open for shipping, although less frequently than they did in the past. In the years since its construction, the Tower Bridge has continued to merit its nickname, "the Wonder Bridge," as it has become an icon of the city of London.

Chapter Four: Symbol of a City

1. Honor Godfrey, *Tower Bridge*. London: John Murray, 1988, p. 49.

2. Quoted in Charles Welch, *History of the Tower Bridge and of Other Bridges over the Thames Built by the Corporation of London*. London: Smith, Elder, 1894, p. 218.

Chronology

1885   The bridge is approved by Parliament and given the Royal Assent.

1886   Construction begins on the piers.

1894   Bridge opens to the public.

1910   The high-level walkways are closed down due to lack of use.

1977   Tower Bridge is painted red, white, and blue to celebrate the queen's silver jubilee.

1982   Tower Bridge opens to the public for the first time since 1910, with a permanent exhibition inside called "the Tower Bridge Experience."

2002   Bridge closes for thirty-nine days as refurbishment work is undertaken.

abutment—A structure that supports the end of a bridge.

bascule—A device or structure, such as a drawbridge, counterbalanced so that when one end is lowered the other is raised; from the French word for "see-saw."

caisson—A watertight structure within which construction work is carried on underwater.

infrastructure—An underlying base or foundation, especially of an organization or system.

pivot—A short rod or shaft on which a related part rotates or swings.

United Kingdom—A country of western Europe that comprises England, Scotland, Wales, and Northern Ireland.

For More Information

Books

Honor Godfrey, *Tower Bridge*. London: John Murray, 1988.

Charles Welch, *History of the Tower Bridge and of Other Bridges over the Thames Built by the Corporation of London*. London: Smith, Elder, 1894.

Web Sites

BBC LDN: London Panoramics (www.bbc.co.uk). British Broadcasting Corporation's Web site, which features panoramic videos of the bridges over the Thames.

Tower Bridge Experience (www.towerbridge.org.uk). Web site for the Tower Bridge history center.

Index

abutments, 17, 28, 29
Armstrong, William, 32

bascule, 6, 13, 14, 17,
    18, 22, 30, 31, 32,
    35, 36, 38, 39, 40, 43
Bessemer converter, 31
Bridge House Estates
    Trust, 39

caissons, 21, 22–23
cantilevers, 27
cars, 40, 41, 43
counterbalance, 30
crown jewels, 11

decorations, 14, 35–36
divers, 20–21
drawbridge, 13

elevators, 13, 27, 35

foundation, 22–23

gaslamps, 35
granite, 35

House of Commons,
    12, 15

Industrial Revolution,
    9–10

Jones, Horace, 5–6, 11,
    13, 14, 19

London Tower Bridge
    challenges of, 10, 12,
        18–20
    cost of, 39
    decorations of, 14,
        35–36
    design of, 10, 12,
        13–14
    foundation of, 22–23
    opening day of, 36,
        38–39
    repairs to, 42–43
    today, 40–43
    traffic on, 39–40, 41

opening day, 36, 38–39

pedestrians, 13, 39–40
piers, 17, 19, 20,
    22–23, 25, 28
pillars, 22, 25-26
pivot, 18, 30
pound sterling, 37, 39
prices, 37

roadway, 6, 17, 23, 30,
    36

safety, 13, 25, 32

scaffolding, 19, 20, 21,
    27
seesaw, 6, 13, 18, 30
steam engines, 14–15,
    18, 30, 31, 32–33,
    35, 36, 40
steel, 11, 14, 18, 25, 27,
    31, 38
suspension chains, 6,
    14, 17, 26, 27–30, 35

Thames River, 5, 9–10,
    12, 13, 18, 20, 38,
    43
Tower Hill, 10, 12
Tower of London, 5,
    11, 14, 35

vibration, 40, 41
Victorian Gothic, 13–14

wages, 37
walkways, 13, 14, 17,
    26, 27, 28, 35, 36,
    39–40, 42
William the Conqueror,
    5, 11
Wolfe-Barry, John
    Wolfe, 14, 19, 33,
    38, 39
Wonder Bridge, 5–7,
    25, 43